D0905121

# THE MAN MADE OF RAIN

# Books available by Brendan Kennelly

POETRY

*The Boats Are Home* (Gallery Press. 1980)
*Cromwell* (Beaver Row, 1983; Bloodaxe Books, 1987)
*Moloney Up and At It* (Mercier Press, 1984)
*Mary* (Aisling Press, 1987)
*A Time for Voices: Selected Poems 1960-1990* (Bloodaxe Books, 1990)
*The Book of Judas* (Bloodaxe Books, 1991)
*Breathing Spaces: Early Poems* (Bloodaxe Books, 1992)
*Poetry My Arse* (Bloodaxe Books, 1995)
The Man Made of Rain (Bloodaxe Books, 1998)

PLAYS

EURIPIDES' *Medea* (Bloodaxe Books. 1992)
EURIPIDES' *The Trojan Women* (Bloodaxe Books, 1993)
SOPHOCLES' *Antigone* (Bloodaxe Books, 1996)
LORCA'S *Blood Wedding* (Bloodaxe Books, 1996)

ANTHOLOGIES

*The Penguin Book of Irish Verse* (Penguin, 1970; 2nd edition 1981)
*Landmarks of Irish Drama* (Methuen, 1988)
*Love of Ireland: Poems from the Irish* (Mercier Press, 1989)
*Between Innocence and Peace: Favourite Poems of Ireland*
    (Mercier Press, 1994)
*Ireland's Women: Writings Past and Present*, with Katie Donovan
    & A. Norman Jeffares (Kyle Kathie/Gill & Macmillan, 1994;
    and Norton, USA)
*Dublines*, with Katie Donovan (Bloodaxe Books, 1996)

LITERARY CRITICISM

*Journey into Joy: Selected Prose*, edited by Åke Persson
    (Bloodaxe Books, 1994)

BOOKS ON BRENDAN KENNELLY

Richard Pine (ed.): *Dark Fathers into Light: Brendan Kennelly*
    (Bloodaxe Books, 1994)
Åke Persson (ed.): *This Fellow with the Fabulous Smile*
    (Bloodaxe Books, 1996)

# The Man Made
# of Rain

**BRENDAN KENNELLY**

BLOODAXE BOOKS

Copyright © Brendan Kennelly 1998

ISBN: 1 85224 454 2  hardback edition
        1 85224 455 0  paperback edition
        1 85224 458 5  complete reading on cassette

First published 1998 by
Bloodaxe Books Ltd,
P.O. Box 1SN,
Newcastle upon Tyne NE99 1SN.


Bloodaxe Books Ltd acknowledges
the financial assistance of Northern Arts.

LEGAL NOTICE

All rights reserved. No part of this book may be
reproduced, stored in a retrieval system, or
transmitted in any form, or by any means, electronic,
mechanical, photocopying, recording or otherwise,
without prior written permission from Bloodaxe Books Ltd.

Requests to publish work from this book
must be sent to Bloodaxe Books Ltd.

Brendan Kennelly has asserted his right under
Section 77 of the Copyright, Designs and Patents Act 1988
to be identified as the author of this work.

Cover printing by J. Thomson Colour Printers Ltd, Glasgow.

Printed in Great Britain by
Cromwell Press Ltd, Trowbridge, Wiltshire.

*For Maurice & Pat Neligan*
*and for*
*David Thomas & Ian Graham*

# ACKNOWLEDGEMENTS

Brendan Kennelly reads the whole of *The Man Made of Rain* on a double-cassette issued by Bloodaxe Books simultaneously with the poem's publication in book form. Thanks are due to John Rowland, Frank Loftus and Trinity College Dublin for help with this recording. Sections of the poem were first read as one of *Five Radio Poems* in BBC Radio 3's *Postscript* series on 30 October 1997.

# NOTE

There are many Englishes within English. These Englishes approach, collide and veer away from each other in startling, perplexing and revealing ways. They enjoy a mind-dazzling variety. There's Dayenglish, for example, and Nightenglish. There's the English of explanation and the calmly ecstatic, dreamenergised English of pure being which has little or nothing to do with the English of good behaviour. Is there a different language for every different emotional planet? In this brief statement, I am applying the language of day to that of night, the language of explanation to the dreamenergised language of being. It is a process we all engage in. We must, in the interests of "communication". It is a civilised process, honest, heartwarmingly ludicrous, and necessary. Reason must worry itself, chew its nails back into its flesh, to explain the dream beyond its reach. If it explains the dream to its own satisfaction, it can tell itself it has the dream in its pocket, snug as a wallet.

I had major heart surgery, a quadruple bypass, in October 1996. The day after the operation I had a number of visions (they probably lasted a few seconds, in daylanguage terms). I saw a man made of rain. He was actually raining, all his parts were raining slantwise and firmly in a decisive, contained way. His raineyes were candid and kind, glowing down, into, and through themselves. He spoke to me and took me on journeys. His talk was genial, light and authoritative, a language of irresistible invitation to follow him wherever he decided to go, or was compelled by his own inner forces to go. Yet he gave no sense of being compelled to do anything, he seemed relaxed in his own freedom, he moved calmly and unstoppably. He led me to different places (I call them 'places') such as my father's grave, inside my father's bones, the land of nolanguage, the place where scars are roads through difficult territories, provinces of history and memory, the place of cold, true cold, and what is that? He took me into brilliant confusions to experience thrilling definitions, or moments of definition. He taught me the meaning of presence, what it means to be truly and fully in somebody's presence, a process of complete dreamsurrender to another's emotional and intellectual reality at its most articulate and vital. He was seeing, hearing and touching phenomena in a way he wished me to imitate so that I might be as real as he. He seemed to want to transfer, frequently with grace and humour, something of his essential being into mine. The interesting thing, now, is that, at this moment, I realise I was stricken in a bed, well, my body was, but I was also involved in a number of odysseys and conversations such as I'd rarely enjoyed or endured in the whole of my health, in the joy of my Dayenglish, in the world of explanation without which education would not exist, the explanation which is meant to make us establish, experience, and propagate the reassuring phenomenon of coherence that guarantees us the right answer to the question: Is it sane to be mad, or mad to be sane?

What is vision? It is completely normal when you're going through it, odd or tricky when you try to speak of it afterwards. The challenge of 'afterwards' is connected with 'afterwords', how to preserve the normality of the visionary moment without being distorted or even drowned in the familiar sea of Dayenglish. If that normality is not kept and sustained, what is sane and true at the moment of experience will come across as bizarre at the moment of telling. And vision is not bizarre though it may witness phenomena that are hair-raising in the telling. Vision, when experienced, is normal as rain falling on trees, grass, gravel, flowers, weeds, streets, people. Vision waits for us, ready to give itself; we use countless techniques to cut ourselves off from it. If I have failed to capture that normality in this poem, then this poem is a flop. If I have been able to suggest that beautiful and intense normality, then this poem may hold some kind of special interest for readers. This depends on how effectively I've persuaded Dayenglish to confront and express nighthappenings. The man made of rain would probably say that if I could surrender to the magical potential of Dayenglish to do the job, then I needn't worry. Nothing seemed to worry the man made of rain. There was a concentrated joy in him. Well, I enjoyed writing this poem in the cold blue winter of 1996-97, just three months after my operation, in Dame Street in Dublin with crowds of young people happily drinking and carousing in the streets all night into early morning, and the man made of rain graciously and deftly flowing through 'afterwards' and 'afterwords' in my mind and imagination. Cold, blue light. Walks along the canal. Cries of lovers or would-be lovers drunk at night, threats and curses flung at the moon. Violence in the streets (you'll see the blood tomorrow), screams of homeless men beating each other up as they headed for favourite doorways or a place in the Saint Vincent de Paul shelter. They sought shelter in the shade of the Saint as I sought to re-create the sheltering, inviting, guiding presence of the man made of rain. In 'afterwards' and 'afterwords', I let these screams invade my being and the paper I wrote on. I wanted to see the dream absorb and transfigure its own violation by the "real". Time is a fierce river and language must do its poor best to keep up with the flow. Let it flow. The man made of rain would not leave me (not that I wanted him to leave me) until I let his presence flow in the best and only poem I could write for him. Though I appear in the poem, or what I recognise as my "own" voice sounds through it, the poem is essentially a homage to his presence, a map of his wandering discoveries, and an evidence of my inadequate witness-ing of those discoveries and that presence. He is a real presence in the poem; I am more an absence longing to be a presence. How, equipped only with 'afterwords', could I possibly do justice to those thrilling voyages, excursions, expeditions, flings, conversations, moments of pure light, and pain that makes vision possible? What I feel now, afterwards, is gratitude to the man made of rain: to his raining light, shining gentleness, flowing sympathy, cheeky piss-taking of my hacked body, his smile inviting me to explore, explore, his pity, compassion, love. Dear man made of rain, dear guide, friend, genial pisstaker, (and whoever else you are), I hope you enjoy this ould poem.

BRENDAN KENNELLY
*December 1997*

# *What?*

'What is my body?' I asked the man made of rain.
'A temple,' he said, 'and the shadow thrown
by the temple, dreamfield, painbag, lovescene,
hatestage, miracle jungle under the skin.

Cut it open. Pardon the apparition.'

'What is my blood?' I dared then.
'Her pain birthing you and me,
the slow transfiguration of pain
into knowing what it means to be

climbing the hill of blood, trawling the poisoned sea.'

'Where have I been when they say I've returned?'
'Where beginning and end
combine to make a picture, compose a sound
reminding you that love is a singing wound

and I could be your friend.'

# THE MAN MADE OF RAIN

# 1

Between living and dying
is the calmest place I've ever been.
He stood opposite me and smiled.
I smiled too, I think, because this was the first time
I'd seen a man made of rain
though once or twice
my heart was chilled by men of ice.
The rain poured through him,
through his eyes, face, neck, shoulders, chest, all his body
but no rain reached the ground,
it ended at his skin.
                    He looked at me with eyes of rain
and said, 'I'll be coming to see you
now and then from this moment on.
Today, I'm colours, all colours.
Look at me, I'll be colours again
but different next time, maybe.
See my colours today.'

I looked. I saw the flesh of rain,
I looked into and through the rain
and saw colours I'd never seen before.
As I looked, the colours began to dance
with each other, some were laughing,
some were crying, some said they were lost
and were looking for their brothers and sisters,
one said he was the colour of work
and it saddened him to see
how easily he made slaves of men.
I looked for the colour of slavery
but couldn't find it. I saw
the colours of poverty instead
like children in O'Connell Street.
'Pick one of us,' they sang in a chorus
'You'll have a friend for life.'
I was indecisive because I was
between living and dying
and anyway the colours
were vanishing into each other

like thoughts that cannot stand alone
but must seek out other thoughts
to stop going mad, why are thoughts
afraid to go mad?
The rain
is laughing at that fear,
I followed the rain of the eyes
and saw the terror
that makes reason necessary
and gives it authority,
an educated terror
that didn't trust the rain.
He never asked me to trust him but I
would trust the man made of rain
to the lip and into the mouth and belly
of eternity, it isn't even a question of trust
more of the kind of interest you find
when you put aside the fear of dying
and look at the light
or listen to the sound of water
or pay attention to pigeons
or her hair when she's unaware
or find yourself swallowing a nightsound
or like the way a scientist talks of ten dimensions.
It is calm in the place beyond trust
and especially calm if you walk there
in the company of your own hurt,
in the company of the man made of rain
pouring beside you
but more contained
than anything in the world
except the pain
waiting at the white door
one cold October evening, leaves falling,
traffic ranting, seagulls hovering,
swooping like dreams
that seek you out
for, it seems,
the fun of it.

O scars of living, the fun those dreams must have!

I won't have to open the door.

He steps forward, opens it, smiles.
I walk in, he vanishes,
nowhere to be seen,
the silver rain is everywhere,
the shadows creep
into the secret corners of the October evening

where live and die
secret and open
dark and light
chaos and wonderplan

are wideawake in the heart of sleep.


## 2


'There are those who'd say you're not normal,'
said the man made of rain.
'Follow me. Better still, walk with me.'

He lifted the pain from me
like you'd lift a cap from your head.
I walked with him.

Always the colours.
Now, the pictures.

A hill.
We climbed it.
I fell.
He picked me up.
There was such strength in the rain
unsuspected strength, the strength of drab,
neglected women and men.

A lime-kiln.
I went down into it.
I tasted the lime.
It changed to fountain-water
that cooled punishment
and made a pact with brutality.

'We'll go to the trees,' he said,
'Now that you know your chest is made of wood.'

The trees talked of folly and cruelty,
they told me of my blindness.
'If you write this down
you'll write it on the death of one
or all of us,' they said.

The man made of rain talked to the trees,
he touched them as he talked,
the trees flourished at his touch,
they were strong as he was gentle.

He cried a little, I think it was
the only time I saw him cry, I'm
wrong, the war between fear and music
draws his tears as well.

That's when he talks of hell.

Look at the children in the field, he said.

| | | |
|---|---|---|
| Tony O'Grady | Teddy O'Sullivan | Séan Creedon |
| Michael Mulvihill | Eddie Joe Dee | Scruffy Grace |
| Billy O'Shea | Noel O'Connell | Paddy Spring |
| Mick Flavin | Jer Enright | Tucker Heaphy |
| Patsy McKibben | Willie Cox | Dropsy Bawn |

changed

to yellow flowers in the green field,
suddenly there was moonlight
and the flowers walked the streets of cities,
flowers out looking for work,
flowers walking streets in moonlight

and the man made of rain called for music,
the flowers danced at his bidding,
yellow flowers dancing in the streets
of New York and London
Liverpool and Boston,
flowers dancing because they'd found work
away far away
from sticks and stones will break my bones
but names will never hurt me
and don't you know
when poverty comes in the door
love flies out the window.

Do not distort me, twist me, misrepresent me,
let me be truthful as the dance,
do not pitch lies at me, or wrap them
like bandages around my mind,

       I am with

the man made of rain, walking with him
through streets of yellow flowers
in the dancing light of exile
where happiness is possible and the edges
of the world are touched by what is gentle.

I hear you say flowers were born for human eyes.
Look into the eyes of the man made of rain.
It is time to go into exile,
pay attention to flowers in exile.
They could turn on each other now,
betray or kill each other

          but not yet.

How hideous that would be, flowers killing each other
like men, like brother killing brother,
like de Valera in Listowel, 'I swear to God,
brothers will wade knee-deep through brothers' blood.'

They did. They do. They will.

Were flowers born for human eyes?

'Look at Callaghan making love to Julie Anne,'
said the man made of rain.

Julie Anne laughs at love, at men,
at Callaghan as she opens her legs
on the floor of Sunday, she laughs
at what he does and thinks, we know
she knows what he thinks
as we stand,
the man made of rain and I,
at the door of the place where coffins are made
for rich and poor and young and old
and love is made
in the light of mockery.

Keep the Sabbath holy but mix love with mockery.

'Here's the fountain,' he said.
'Callaghan is a flower in New York,
Julie Anne is a flower begetting flowers
in a small house down a side-road in Limerick
and you're a flower with thoughts making noise
in your head. I can hear them rattling.

When humans look at flowers,
flowers bear the burden of the eyes
that they enrich.'

The fountain leaped like a young goat,
the man made of rain mingled with it,
the fountain knelt in homage,
it told him its troubles, it asked him
to pray for the water of the world, the water
is threatened,

                    I see the rain
in the man's heart, no poison there,
I see the rain composing his hair
relaxed and pure, I see
the rain pouring down his body
into his legs, pouring like grace
from head to toe, out to the edge
of his fingers, through his teeth
when he smiles.

He smiles. 'Wherever I am
is peace. Peace does not belong
to the dead alone.'

The fountain rejoices, back on its feet.
The water pours through his head
like questions through an eager child.

Why is peace so threatening to some?
Why do they try to strangle it?
Break its back and legs with clubs and hammers?
Why are they afraid to see it grow?

'You're slow,' he said, 'So slow, painfully,
pitifully slow.'

I know.

And yet I thought I moved.
I believed I moved.
Lord, that I may walk.

My pillow feathers whisper I'm made of lead.

That I may walk.

'There are those who'd say you're not normal,' he said.

# 3

'When you walk through my tongue
you're in a land of no language,' he said.

He opens his mouth, I walk in,
I wander through the tongue of rain.
I don't expect to meet such innocence again,
innocence that is, as I understood it then.

Are there words for innocence?
Let witnesses come forward.

Half-way through the tongue I see Dan Conners
push Mrs Morrisey's bread from her windowsill
                    into her backyard muck,
then hide behind a bush to hear her cry.
She has ten children to feed and what will feed them this night?

I did nothing about it.
I said nothing.

The tongue of rain is licking my mind.

I'm under it now, looking up.

He says it's a land of no language but I see
shadows of words running off his tongue,
word-shadows flicker and sway,
stop as if startled, then flow

in a river of silence through the tongue of rain.
I think I know what he means now,
this is before the first word is born,
anxious and puzzled, alone, pleadingly simple,
tense on the threshold of saying

or singing.

All that I say and am and can be
comes after,
but is born then.

At the back of his tongue, I see rooms
where they whimper and cry, men and women unheard.
Who is their word?
Where may it be found?
I taste his silver spittle, the blood of words
in the veins of the rain in his mind.

In the land of no language
I beg understanding of shadows,
I look, listen, wait to be born
in a word on the tip of the tongue
where I wander forever,
a guest at the feast of silence
soon to return to the room where I lie
conscious (they say), scarred and still,
pigignorant of words I kill.

**4**

I said,   'There's no way
       I could ever say
       you.'

       'Say I'm the air's notebook.
       Birds jot their thoughts on my pages.'

       'Have I the neck?'

       'Say I'm the heart-attack
          Jupiter survived. Say
       Elvis reached Jupiter
          in less than an hour.'

       'Can I believe that, even
          in the light of my end?'

       'Say I'm the lost spirit-currency
             you found
             and are learning to spend.

       'Say I could be your friend.'

# 5

'You're dying tonight,' said the man made of rain.

'What can I do?' said my blood.

He understood.

'There are two mushrooms growing
under the tree outside your window.'

'Should I turn mushroom?'

'You might give it a shot.'

> Anxious leaves, plastic bags,
> envelopes, newspapers, birthday cards,
> rubber tyres and a clothes hanger
> rustled I was dying.

But he whispered, 'Dear mushroom,
for the moment, you're not.'

Moment. For the moment. I'm not.

I see a house with a red roof
close to the hill of blood
that I must climb
wearing my favourite boots.
Will the man of rain accompany me?
Loneliness is a special kind of company,
it'll go anywhere with me, I don't have to ask it,
I can feel it close to my heart,
snuggling in there,
feathery, not rough, but with a kind
of cold tenderness I find
nowhere else.

I'll never forget these mushrooms
in late October.

The things that keep you alive
on the brink of November,
month of the dead where I come from.


I turn away from the hill of blood
and talk to the mushrooms.
They've had their own growing problems
but are enjoying maturity.
So would I if I ever reached it.
What is it?
Don't give me a cautious answer.


It is my stricken guess
that more men die of caution
than excess.


'Keep on talking,' he says. He's here.
'Keep on talking. You're among your own.'

The mushrooms don't object.

I'm drifting in a sea of warm blue oil,
I've been drifting for years, mushrooms
at my side, whispering, I'm listening,
I've never heard of dying here in this
oily sea of blue, suddenly there are
heads everywhere, bobbing, asking me
questions, voraciously bidding me welcome,
home at last, home, warm blue home,
no fear of drowning, that's over, where am
I from, am I alone, where did I learn
how to drift like this without a care,
in or out of the world, same thing, drifting,
the heads are singing to me and a woman
with a basket of flowers tells me to sleep
in the sea, I'm the sea's child, so sleep,
sleep in the sea, the clothes hanger rustles
says nothing, the anxious leaves are starting
to relax where they drift, broken and free.

If this is drowning, drowning's for me.

# 6

'So what if blood runs down the hillside,
it'll come home in time,' he said.

'It's mine,' I said. 'That blood is mine
and it's running all over the bloody place.'

'Right you are,' he said. 'And it's no harm
if you stain the green green grass now and then.
Mix the colours like women and men.
Some men never see their blood, is it
any wonder they're so keen to shed the blood
of others, some of the worst evil is spread
by men who've never seen their own blood
spilled.'

The rain poured through his forehead, shining,
I could see his brain, it was bigger
than America, dark as Ireland and necessary
as the old enemy so loved in ways. The rain
falling through the brain was itself the brain
and was light as praise
                    touching
                        a child's head.

'Let me show you your blood,' he said.

'Some other time,' I answered. 'I'm too busy
dying right now.'

'You're full of excuses,' he said.
'But all right, I'll wait.'

He started to climb the hillside
the blood coming against him parted
and he walked the green path
not bothering to look back.

Blood on either side
he conquered the hillside.
The sun shone through the blood
the blood shone through him
but was no part of him,
it was a spectator, fifty thousand spectators
waiting
to pummel heaven with excited cries.
He let the blood be,
he let the blood flow
whichever way it chose or dared to flow
or was compelled to flow.

He reached the hilltop, stood alone
in the climbing light.

Shining, he was shining, maker and mover,
he laughed like rain in May, big drops
that land chuckling on your shoulders,
big generous drops, he sparkled, his brain
a storm of light in my darkness,
he stood at the top of the hill, shining,
free and easy, top of the hill.

In my vilest ignorance, in my cage of blood,
I see him still.

## 7

'Freedom is wings,' he said.

We passed Ballyseedy Cross, eight out of nine
blown to pieces.

'The German loves his mother,' he said.
'The cottage was lost and found in Cavan
of the jokes, not forgetting Kerry, mind you,
you will mind yourself, won't you, promise
me that, an' bless yourself goin' out the door,
never know what you're lettin' yourself in for.'

The man made of rain began to flow,
this flowing was for the pain that must
be forgotten, mustn't it?

> This flowing meant changes
>    in the old castles
>       the new estates
>          the bag on the thief's back
>             the old woman planning
>                a walk before Wednesday
>                   the seven flowers
>                      transfiguring the room
>                         in the house on the road
>                            to nowhere.

It happened we were passing another house.

'That's a safe house,' he said. 'Killers rest there.
Murder must find a place to lay its head.'

'Jesus,' he said, 'the sadness of traffic.
The plight of people going places.'

There were nine flowers now.
There was a grey wall, had once been white,
love and sweetness through the night.

'Only when he sings is he real,' he said,
pointing to the young man advising
children how to go to hell pleasantly,
for a while, anyway.

'There are no brief visits to hell,' he said.
'I have a letter here, it's from a young man
drowned in America, he loved the sea, it
invited him, betrayed him, he knew he was free,
he writes of diving into childhood, it felt
like flying.'

I see the young man diving in his brain.
I hear the sea, the whispers, sighs.
I see the young man diving through his eyes.
You'd think he was flying.
Freedom is wings.

I can only repeat what I see.
I cannot say why
what I see
flows through me.
Eyes see what they see, that's history.

He sits in a chair in a corner of the room now.

'You might live,' he says.

I love the hint of laughter in the light about his head.

Put a head in the light, it displaces the light,
how does the light feel?
Does the light know the meaning of revenge?
The wild justice of striking back?
Has the light a history of dispossession?
I want to read the history of light
but that's a history no one made of flesh can write.

The laughter of the man made of rain
is the envy of people and books.
It's a sound like all the promises
chance or man or God makes it possible to fulfil.

It's a light striding sound,
a childrunner in the blood,
loving every moment of being,
its own being, mine, yours too.

Mary Ann Callaghan puts her hands on her hips,
laughs till her false teeth dangle
and her pension book threatens
to fall in the mud and the dust
where Keonach sells the Dingle mackerel
on the grounds that if you eat this fish
you'll find wisdom and a job in Dublin.

'Sure the Salmon of Knowledge is only
trottin' after it,' Keonach laughs,
cool silvery shillings in his hand.

'Eat fish from Dingle, fish from Dingle,
you'll be the brightest in the land.'

'Don't worry if you lose sight of me,' says
                            the man of rain,
'Something of me lingers
where I am not.'

He raises his hand, I am transfixed
by rain that composes his fingers.

It stretches away to the end of the world,
the edge of things, is there an edge?
It is closer to me than my own heartbeat.
He has perfect fingers,

fingers of silver rain, all light and shining,
don't blame me if I think of paradise,
yes, the fingers contain a garden
where love walks and meditates on all
that is not itself but may yet be part
of itself, I see a man
beautiful and blameless walking through
*I papaveri*, they are a revolution
against the grey conspiracies of swamps
oozing into the minds of men.

The hill of blood rebels against the swamps.

The garden vanishes.

There are flowers in his fingers.

I count them with all I know of love.


Ten.


One for bones and flesh
two for school
three for a bright lad
four for a fool
five for glad giving
six for peace
seven for loving

in a ruin made of stories

eight for children laughing in the eyes
of strangers to each other
till the moment flashes

nine for silence
the bequest of pain

ten for the music

of the man of rain.

# 8

Amor.
A man of rain.
Nobody intended that.
Yet he had to happen.
When he happened my world outgrew itself.

He is not born of intention.
He is what must happen.
He never heard of reason.
If he did, he pities it.

How do I know that?
Is the rain longing to be human?
Is there a human somewhere
longing to be rain?

A human being
longing
to flow forever,
to pour forever, yet be contained,
to fall on houses anywhere,
on first love, last words,
plans hatched in darkness,
bloody murder, fields of wheat
ripening through summer days

      longing to fall
         like blessings

           like praise.

# 9

'Let's go for a walk through your scars,' invited
                                    the man of rain.

Away we went.

Half-way down my chest, he headed for an old castle,
climbed to the top and said 'You played love here
when you were seventeen. Nobody heard your words
but herself and the Shannon
and maybe a few seagulls on their way to Clare.'

Seventeen. What have I done? Where have I been?

He pointed to blood on a street.
'That's where Moriarty and yourself were beaten up,'
he said. 'That was the first and only time you saw
a mystic with a black eye and a broken jaw.'

A long stretch of road then. Calm. Small birds in hedges.
'I love it when the small birds sing,' he said.

I saw my scars becoming roads in his rainy head,
I saw small birds in cages, singing with such ecstasy
you'd swear to heaven they were wild and free.

'You filled two pints of Guinness for Jackie Carroll the night
he was killed,' he said. 'There's the small cross
to his memory.' I looked. A small cross.
All around, the soft implacable grass.

The next stretch festered. 'You were lost here,' he said.
'You were lonely and mean, your heart black as tar.'
Four o'clock in the morning, a woman is crying,
I don't know where I'm going but I go that road
because that's what roads are for, I bear
witness to this festering scar.

Travelling a hacked body is a healthy adventure.

Roads. Walked on. Driven on. Trampled. Used
like some of the women in the village I grew up in.
I want to listen to the voices of the roads,
voices of my scars, now more than ever I know
few voices are heard on this babbling stage.

Let go. Listen. Let go.

In the freedom of being lost, I hear choked voices flow.

'This road leads to a yellow house on a hill.
A woman taught you here. Try not to lie, she said.
She loved you. She's gone. So is the house. You see them still.'

I do.

He sees I'm tiring. 'Rest,' he says. 'Rest here.'
I fall asleep near a deep scar,
a thin, healing road of blood.

He walks away.

When I wake, I'll go back the roads I came.
I'll meet the hearts. A heart is laughing, a heart
is calculating, a heart grieves, a heart wonders,
a heart rages.

Jackie Carroll. Two pints the night he died.

What did the seagulls hear
on their way to Clare?

What is love in a yellow house on a hill?

Try not to lie.

Small birds sing in cages,
sing with such ecstasy
you'd swear that they were wild and free.

# 10

He pleaded   'Let me happen to you.
                 Let me happen to you.'

It was a time when I'd no words.

        I watched him

        climbing a house
           opening a window
                rescuing a man
                    from himself.

The man of rain brought the man of flesh
                down to earth
                    where he belonged
                        and laid him in the arms
                        of his brother

        who thought he was lost.

The man of rain walked off down the road
                that became a scar
                that became a river
                that became a line
                    of poetry

                burning

                in his brain.

I saw the line of poetry burning in his brain,
                burning in the water of his brain.
                The water was on fire
                  and the line turned cool
            in the middle of the fiery water
                still burning like revenge.

Amid burning revenge, one cool line of poetry.

On he walked, water and fire and poetry
               ready to rescue anyone
                    trapped in himself
                         and return him
                              to his brother.

It was a time when I'd no words
               but I let him happen
                    to me as he
                         had pleaded

and he poured through me
               with a look
                    with a smile
                         with a line

not mine, although I witness it, not mine.

The words are returning like workers from exile,
some of them want to tell me their stories,
               I want to listen,
the words of workers in exile will be mine
                    and I will let them sink
                         into the darkness
                              where blood begins to think
                                   of all that blood is not
                                        but

                         thanks to pain

                         may be

                              yet.

# 11

A Dublin gangster,
now retired,
living with a hammer,
a mother, her daughter,
is hammering nails into my chest
which has of late become a block of wood.
As he hammers, he prays
my soul will find eternal rest
in the light of the mercy of God.
'You'll travel many a road,' he says
'Before you meet a gangster like me.'

I agree

yet wonder
how a brilliant Sunday paper
might decipher
how this gangster
relates
to a hammer
a mother
her daughter

and how the mercy of God
might make its sweet forgiving way

through a block of wood.

# 12

The man who said he was terrified
by the silence of the infinite spaces
must have looked through the eyes
of the man of rain.

Yet it is necessary to go beyond terror
and if you persist in looking through those eyes
you find a state of such clarity
peace is happy to live in you.

All words spoken and written
are drops of rain falling from a seagull's wings.
All the books are the forgotten famine dead
and no one knows the words of their song.

This in itself could be a source of the terror
but this too vanishes in that clear state
where the bones of all your dead foregather
to greet and welcome you, set you at your ease.

The creation of terror is a coward's art
and when I terrify myself by looking
at what I cannot begin to understand
I pray to be rain on a seagull's wings

falling on my cowardice creating terror
as a way out, a solution, to the eyes
of the man of rain looking through me
being looked through, seen, known, so what?

Think, say the eyes, of the beauty of nothing ;
call it the cheetah's speed or the Nine o'clock News,
the Weekend Supplement or Shakespeare in a nutshell,
a one-legged pigeon or a bubbly Millennium.

The beauty of nothing celebrates all the lost books,
the empty libraries of the infinite spaces,
words wandering, comets, lost starving children
whose eyes possess your eyes,

their silence saying, look into the eyes of the man
made of rain, cries of the victims of terror,
light on wet slates, the pain of admitting nothing
is the passion and the logic of beginning.

Meg Murphy is five. Eyes wide. 'I *lo-o-ve* reading!'

# 13

When I see a word
vanishing
into the rain of his head
I see a hand
shaping the word
'beginning'.
My eyes of a man
of flesh
explore the eyes of a man
of rain
and I see
there is no beginning,
no end.
There is a now
that cannot be grasped
so let me invent
my past
my future
to stop me knowing
the radiant nothingness
of now,
the drugged pain
of now,
the terrifying speed
of now
all through my slow carcass,
my slow soul.
This little now
is so beyond me
I'd better make haste
to invent
eternity.
Stranger at my door,
help me.

It was nice of death to stand aside a while
and make a little space, not much
but enough for me to see

a man beating a woman to death
with a red brick,
the kind of brick

lauded for the part it plays
in certain forms of architecture.
I'd read about such bricks

in smashing books, their epic
elegance filling my mind for days.
The red brick bashed the woman

till her spirit rebelled through her battered head
and passed through the veins
of the man made of rain

standing nearby.
Her clear spirit began its adventure
in the knowledge it would never die

but wander forever through veins and eyes
deeper than Homer's sea.
Feathers of gossip have a similar agility

and power of endurance
but nothing in her spirit was sick.
I saw it journeying. I saw the man with the brick

standing over her body in the shadow
of a gorgeous Cathedral renowned
in this city for the crowning of an English King

who approved of the music that evening.
The man with the brick was blind
to the man made of rain,

blind to almost everything, in fact.
He stood where death had created a space
for me, grim guilt on his face,

the Cathedral bells starting to toll,
the future plotting its revenge
in a small corner of the murderer's soul.

Otherwise, he was free to go, more or less.
The man of rain watched him hurry down Waterloo Road.
He watched her body too, the brick dumped near her head.

He carried her within him, gently as he could.

# 15

'Who's to say if you're sane or insane?'

'A normal man.'

'Who can say what it means to be a normal man?'

'I can.'

'Do, then.'

'I can't.
If I did
you might think I was mad.'

# 16

I look at rain pouring through him,
never breaking the skin,
just pouring in that world of light
visible behind skin, transparent man,
nothing to hide, I think of all our
hidden sicknesses, poems made of lies, skilful
things, fodder for prizes, consolatory,
ethical, I see him lucid, a man
of quiet clarity, pouring, contained,
who is the patron saint of rain?

Mary Ann Callaghan would be the woman
to answer that
and dare I disbelieve her?

"'Tis all them clouds you have to thank for rain,'
        says Mary Ann,
"Specially the black wans with the snarly faces.
Them bastards is your patron saint.'

I saw him once stuff clouds into his pocket.
He reached up, gathered a crop of clouds,
white, grey, some black as anger,
put them in an inside pocket, I could
see through them, even the black ones,
they had fragments of the world in them,
oppressing them, I thought, weighing them down
but after a while he took the clouds
out of his pocket, threw them back in the sky
where they stretched themselves
like waking greyhounds,
and went for a race
delighted to be free.

To see delighted clouds enjoying themselves
shot fun through me.

I could have died with the thrill
of that shooting fun.

I thought for a moment I'd love to be
a cloudy man

but I was tied to a bed,
pumps sticking out of me.
You look a bit ridiculous, the pillowfeathers said.

He gets on well with clouds
but doesn't like to see them get too gloomy.
The gloomy ones slump in the sky
like bags under people's eyes,
sad and heavy and full
of poison waiting
to ooze into the eyes
and blind the people.
He doesn't like to see that happen.
He likes the clouds that move
and frisk a little in their freedom
like terrier pups
or lion cubs
or little leopards learning how.
The sky is a place of learning
and clouds should make the most of light,
kicking up their heels in their blue playground,
frolicking with heaven
never letting it get too serious
'cos all the gods are longing to smile
but men of flesh won't let them.

How may the gods escape
important, gloomy men?

I think if I had made the world
I'd smile, now and then.

My blood is happy when I stand
and look at clouds.

And is there anything more sweet and sane
than to lie
between living and dying

and listen to the rain?

# 17

It was a long time afterwards
  (after what? please don't switch on the light)
I heard one of my father's bones say
  'An epic is one word explored
    like the inside of a bone,
  explored until it's glad to surrender
  secrets of highabove deepwithin downunder.
    One word alone. Take
  the word of an old man's bone.'

I take your word for it, fatherbone.
  Who knows the loneliness of words,
thin, drifting flames in the infinite cold?
  I am the child of a lost language
though I've run into it all over the world
  and it runs through me now and then.
...*agus ni baoghal duit an ragairne*...
  The ragairne stonecrushes my head tonight
(it must be night, please let it be night),
          the ragairne
lashes the island until all I can do is leave it,
          curse it
in words that never have enough of the lash,
  let me live in an icy corner of Asia,
swim through the darkness of the epic Asian night.
Ragairne. Asia. I listen to him.
One word. Enough to eat my life. Darkness.
        Switch on the light.

# 18

Birds of pain hover about my bed this darkness
singing their dark song to my rubbled flesh.
I taste the masterful blackbird, the gritty yellowhammer,
              the passionate thrush

                    celebrating
                    my wish,

              my trapped yet flying wish.


# 19

Everyone on this island knows everything that may be known
              about rain.
There'd be a noticeable decline in life-giving talk if heaven
              sent us less rain.
Many muttered blessings and curses are the children
              of rain
         and I know one sparkling woman who loves
              to make love in the rain.

(Jesus, says Mary Ann Callaghan, is it any wonder
         she'll be crippled with arthritis
              when she's only forty-wan!)

# 20

What's the weight of flesh in the world just now?
The question bobbed in my mind like a red
ball in water at the foot of a monument

I know or remember or made up
in order to keep my grip on things.
First, you have these five continents

huge yet small enough when you place them
in atlaswater ; they contain much flesh
with millions of tons more on the way

because we love each other, that's what we say,
or slip into bed or get a good ride
or enjoy feast and speeches with bridegroom and bride.

Even as it burns to ashes or merges with clay
flesh is replaced by promising cries
and new names chosen most lovingly.

What's the weight of it? Weight of it all?
Heavy heavy heavy despite
testosterone, epitestosterone, what you will

and the earth bears it all with a grin
of winter or spring, bears millions of tons
of flesh sleeping and waking, flesh of men,

women, children, flesh everywhere, all the time,
flesh making flesh, killing flesh, loving flesh,
punishmentbeating flesh, being born is the crime

and the sentence is living, the mad Dean said.
I lay beyond living, still trying
to calculate the weight of the dead

before I'd advance on the problem of now,
the living, bless them all days, all ways.
I'd like mathematics to learn how to fly

beyond the proveable, it will, one day,
meanwhile the man of rain sits
on the edge of the bed, he suggests

a flick of the brain from flesh to rain,
from solid to flowing, I try to comply,
a needle is gossiping in my blood,

you dirty old thing you dirty dirty old thing.
Well, proveable enough, let the gossip flow,
the man of rain is smiling,

I know that smile, he's taking the side
of flesh right now, backing the way it is
supporting the way we flourish and rot from day

to day, that's the secret, out in the open,
but nothing's out in the open, not completely, his smile
supports that too, it's a necessary style,

he always has mercy on style which must
exist if flesh is to continue
its long adventure through bone and sinew,

itself, as it is, now. Let me lie here and think
till I sleep or imagine I sleep a wink
and fly or imagine I fly when flesh

would have me sink.

There's no edge, only a new place with
one side veering away into nothing and
Mary Moroney is kindness itself, all care
loving care, turns over that body anytime
day or night.

Colours of the left leg, cut from ankle to groin
or groin to ankle if you prefer, I like
ankle to groin for reasons I'll not go into here,
invade the head and capture
three major cities
with the convinced skill of Oliver Cromwell
my old foepal for whom I received
a whack on the jaw on O'Connell Bridge
the night after I mentioned to Gaybo
Oliver had a lot going for him
and we could do with a visit now.
He'd show the killers how to behave so he would,
he'd take the shine off their bliss,
he'd lay down the law, the Lugs Branigan.

Black yellow red brown and
a vaguely disgusting white
are the colours of my left leg.
They hurtle into each other like dirty footballers,
you'd swear my colours wanted to knock each other out,
I was white once, or as white as the next Paddy,
the only thing to do when you're backward is
let yourself fly, I'm blueredblackyellowbrown
                and I don't mind it at all
so don't give it a thought if you see me cry.

I never thought I'd see the day
when I'd cry like the rain
and not begin to know why.

Truth is the tears I can never explain.

Say I'm buried, say I'm on show somewhere,
on exhibition in Merrion Square,
a postmodern explosion of latent rebellions,
Handy Andy from New York would enjoy me
and I haven't even been bombed
or expelled from my province
to become a sly colonising refugee
with a genius for eliciting sympathy.
I haven't cut off my ear
or jumped off a bridge
or distinguished between essential and obvious
because here you could take these labels
turn them upside down for a laugh
and find the battle of the colours
going on in my skin
in that room in the Gallery
where they hang masterpieces
like Judas moving in for the kiss
discovered in old Jesuits' bedrooms
or Big Houses down the country
the IRA forgot to burn
or was it the other lads?
Someone will burn them some day,
            don't worry your head.

Black yellow brown red
blood on the pillow

a woman in my bed
where did she come from?

It was like a tractor going over your body,
says Shirley Love
with the angeltouch.

Massey Ferguson was my favourite tractor,
treacherous bastards tractors are,
plough you into the ground in no time at all
when you wouldn't be looking
with nothing but the green green
grass of home for company
and a trickle of red, you wonder
a moment what is the source of red,

red red who called it red,
woman nowoman in my bed?

Eyelids fall.

The colours are even clearer now
and a few new ones
have joined the company.
These new ones were born in the mind of snow
but they never honoured me till now.

O the colours of pain
are enough to make me dance
at a feis in a field
between Asdee and Ballybunion.

Dance, sing the colours, dance
till he comes, man of rain
whose colours the rainbow envies.

He looks at the colours of my left leg,
touches them, they start to change
into the colours of each other,
Jews into Arabs, Arabs into Jews,
Ulster Protestants into Ulster Catholics
and vice versa, making new colours,
no words for them, not yet, no words
needed they flow
like trout like eels in the Feale,
there is no edge, only this new place

where I am real, real

            as my colours
                in late October
                    with leaves falling

            and Dermot Gillespie
                in the next bed
                    breathing,

        against all the evidence

                breathing.

# 22

Come into the ground with me now, he says.

I follow.

I'm in my father's grave, the man of rain
picks up a bone and hands it to me.
'You love that, don't you,' he says
'It always loved you.'

I hold my father's bone in my hand.
A fair ould worker when he wanted to be,
could take a faulty clock to pieces
and put it together again. Perfect.
His hands on her dark head. Singing.

*When first I saw you on the village green.*

Fixed tractors too. Massey Ferguson.
In the earth all this time. How long? Strong bone.
Damp earth. Isn't it always raining
in North Kerry, that's where the snipe
wear wellingtons and swallows from Africa
swim through the summer.

I see his other bones now.

The man of rain stands silent by.
'Whenever I hear McCormack, my bones are fit to sing,' he said.

My father's bones are fit to sing.
I hold them in my hand.
I smell. Inhale. Hail, full of stories.

His life electrifies my darkness,
Scrolm Hill, the Civil War, America,
whiskey in Ballybunion with Jackie Boland,
the pouring, pouring stories.

A man must fight the hours his heart is lonely.

Bones and stories.

It's raining in my father's grave.

Blue Shannon light accommodates the rain.

I run my fingers over the bone, it's
cold to the touch, it warms my heart,
have another Gold Flake,
sixty a day, is it any wonder
I need the pace-maker, Bridie, is it
any wonder I cough my heart up
every morning, the mad thumping, but I'd
rather one Gold Flake than a
fortnight in Florida. They'll kill
me yet, I s'pose. The ould heart.

*Come to me e'er my dream of love is o'er.*

I can't stop them, not that I'd want to
but the bones in my hands are singing.

I'm following the man of rain
round and round my father's grave
inside deepdown inside
through his bones, deep within his bones.

Deeper than Ireland, wider than America
is this grave,
here's my journey now, I have my guide,
I follow the man of rain, he moves
like the summer of '55 every moment
bright and warm, touching me
without touching me, leading me
through the dark inside of my father's bones,
dark passages of laughter love smoke
stories phrases like the night in the kitchen
'I wish to Christ I was dead,'
and I never asked why,
why did I never ask why?

Nor will I ask why
his bones are singing now

I will never ask it of myself
I will never ask another human
I will never ask the air or the earth to explain.


I'll follow the man of rain
leading me through my father's bones,
the roads within,
the games, the wars, the ways of neighbours,
the scars that might say something
of what I've done, people I've hurt
been hurt by, strange places I've been,
believed I've been.

*When you were sweet, when you were sweet sixteen.*

He'd two daughters, six sons, I'm walking
through his skull, its mountains
glens valleys narrows caves
in Ballybunion where a father and son
went to explore between tides
and never returned though a car
was waiting to take them home.

I climb the walls of a cave in his skull
and hear the wild white horses
bellowthreatening a few yards away, it seems.

Once upon a time, his dreams ran through this cave.
If my dreams met his,
here, now,
how would they get on together?

Would they talk to each other?

I'm climbing now and come upon
three gates, I open each one
and am able for the mountain
taller than his forehead
when I saw him first.

Darkness next, I go through that
flicking now and then the lamp he gave me
to see if the cow had calved in the shed.

The skull is the least dead road I've travelled,
nothing but surprise
behind where used to be his eyes.


I look and see the eyes
of the man made of rain
looking through my father's eyes.

Love shines through death,
kisses it with those eyes.
Death has its own answer,
its only answer.
Love kisses death again, again.
Death disappears
in the eyes of rain.

I'd love to turn on my left side
but cannot.
I might as well be nailed to the sheet
damp with my sweat.

Lie there in the arms of pain.
Could this be forever?

He's gone.

Father.

Son.

Why can't I lie on my left side?

Where are you, man made of rain?

Beyond all wonder is a wonderplan
combining blue and white
with the raucous threats and curses
of the night

Shadows scale a red wall
a man calls for peace
a boy and a girl kick down a door
in Thomas Street

Inside my skin four rows of birds
prepare for flight
Wherever they go I wish them well
I'm glad we met

Beyond all wonder is a wonderplan
I'll see it if I will
Jack Kilready is a dying man
so are we all

dying into wonder beyond wonder
beyond blue and white beyond peace
beyond killers of peace beyond
loss beyond all fear of loss

The poison in my body
is the poison of my time.

Kill the trees, kill them here, anywhere,
feed the poison to the paper,

feed the paper to the eyes,
feed the eyes with ugliness.

Killing follows killing follows killing.
The only thing to fear is healing.

Young murderer licks sweat off my thighs
devours the checkpoint with his eyes.

Feed the eyes feed the eyes.
Someone's in for a surprise.

Soldier is nearly twenty-three,
bit young for hell or heaven, too

old for earth, earth's poison
raving through me this stone afternoon.

Bullet wipes away young man.
Murderer licks my sweat again
keen to glut himself on poison.

He can never get enough, failed murderous glutton.
Where is she? Would she recognise her son,
very pretty lad assassin?

I'm poisoned father poisoned brother
murdered man and his murderer

together we've betrayed the sun
the sun's revenge is heaven's poison

my own

# 25

The accent crawls, colonising the loch,
practising itself in the still
evening.
      Slithery as a snake, rooted as a rock,
it knows how to whine, flatter, beg, kill.


# 26

Hacked, bruised, foul. 'What is flesh?' I asked the man of rain.
'A kind of everything waiting to be nothing,' he said.
'Great worker, best servant on earth, dustpoem,
lovething, vivid presence in the process of vanishing.'

'Where does it vanish to?' I asked.

He smiled, started walking.

I wanted to rise and follow quickly
but something heavier than the world prevented me,

whispering, Stay, you cannot do without me.

## 27

'I've never seen you before,' I said,
though I knew I had.
On the hill of blood.

'That may be true,' he said, 'but you see me now,
this cold blue bright day.'

His eyes' cold blue light is
what history should be,
so clear
it makes fleshcomplexity look sad.

Have you been here before, I wondered, will you
be here again?

He read my silent wondering.

'I haven't much time for tenses,' he replied.

My flesh is hot and thick.

Past, present, future. The three-card trick.

Greyhound racing in Glin.
'Pick your card,' the gambler said.
I did and as I did
I knew I'd lost.

Three cards on a table
in a field where the hounds
neck in for the kill. Three cards.
Past, present, future.
The hare's cry is with me still.
No cry like the cry of a gentle creature.

Another gambler said, 'There's a fourth card
you can learn to play.
There's always another card.'

The eyes of the man of rain
outshine the light of the cold blue day.
I throw all the cards away.

He opens up the late October sky.
Windy. Every leaf that flies and falls

is a hare's cry.

I don't propose to go on about cries
but I've been hearing a lot of them lately,
mainly from within.

They need to be heard, I'd say.
But most leaves blow away
or are carted away
to a hole outside Arklow
in the Garden of Ireland.

I'm walking among the cries
buried in the Garden of Ireland.
Nobody gets in touch, nobody writes
to the cries or inquires after them
like 'Is it true you nearly died?'
The cries are shy. If such questions were asked
they'd hardly be answered.

Maybe a cry is question and answer all in one.

The loneliest cry I ever heard
was from an Indian woman
who'd lost her handsome, arrogant son.

No, not quite the loneliest.

Thy will be done.

How lonely was God
when he decided
to make a man

who'd cry
like that?

# 28

Major operations on the body
operate the mind.

At twenty past four
the godesses let their waters flow.
Stories of long ago.

The black bar ramming three white clouds
is a wound gone underground.

Up on the ditch he set me
when I was nine,
stuck his hand up my trousers,
his black eyebrows scorching me
his tongue licking his turfy lips.

'Did you bring me any black Bendigo tobacco?' he asks.
'I love it, 'tis the devil to cut though I have
the wickedest little knife in the world.'

His hands are calm and mad.
Sit still on the ditch, don't scream,
his black eyebrows fester with rats.

Paddy Brolley traps me between his legs.
He's eighty years of age, I'm eight,
he's laughing, his knees bang me,
manipulating,
coddin' is what he'll call it
if I start screaming.

'Now I have you trapped.
You'll never escape.'

More than half a century later
I'm trapped between his legs.

His old penis twitches like a rat in his grey trousers.

His laughter is a cage as well.
Paddy Brolley is a bit o' hell,
the bones of his knees are digging into my eyes
my mind is bleeding, he's laughing, why
is blood always surprising,
is the pillow drenched, are the feathers protesting?

What can I do
but let blood flow
like memories of long ago
that are the living now,
madcap antics, love, hate, rage,
rob Collins's orchard, run, hide, eat
the apples under the bridge, quick,
there's a comin' tide.

Tonight, I'm trapped in a cage.

No coddin'.

Mindbleeding never ends.

What's half a century between friends?

Now is then, then is now,
no such thing as long ago.

In the stillness of the night
in the prone silence of the body
I know
the fierce uncontainable flow

of the gentle eyes
of the man of rain.

It is part of me tonight,
this high springtide of blood
lifting in its rising hands
images
I cannot hide.

How much have I hidden?

How much have I lied?

Give me the courage
to rise and flow with the tide.


I can't see him but I know
he's standing out there
in here
in the darkness
in my mind

at my side.

# 29

The man of rain walks the streets of Dublin.

Shadows are candid beside him, behind
and before.

O'Connell Street of the crimes he loves,
drinks it with his eyes,
seagulls crapping on the Liberator.

The Liffey is bullockthick.
How can it ever flow like him?

Beaten children beaten women freezing men
murdered prostitutes and their crying parents
seek refuge in the cool lucid nowhere
visible through his skin.

As he walks, the unacknowledged victims
walk through him.
Dignity lives in his welcoming rain.

Shadows gather to salute, pay him homage,
solid bodies walk unresolved,
trapped in their solidity.

So they live, the bulkythick
and the flowing inescapable nothings
walking through each other.

If I cannot say what I see
have I seen it?

If I see it
do I believe it?

If I believe it
do I twist it
with my scarred mind?

I can only give the smithereens I find.

The man of rain walks the streets of Dublin
like a giant flower
the unacknowledged generations
have slaved to create.
This flower is a human poem
the trodden streets can read.
This poem is the hope of doorways
the whine of midnight traffic
the midair scrawks of seagulls
can you spare me fifty pence, sir, please
and may God bless you and yours forever.

Only in nowhere may I plead for nothing.
Dublin is a buzzing nowhere.
Strange how the flowing blood can freeze.

Fifty pence, sir, please. Please.

The human poem turns away from the lit streets
to walk the dark graffiti
of menace longing condemnation and despair.

I follow, place my trust in nowhere.
Nowhere takes it, fondles it like a small red ball.
Nowhere, the only home that welcomes all.

The tree at my window is October.
I spread my fingers in the hospital air.

Mary Moroney, love and care,
turns me on my side

from which perspective I see
        the man of rain
            the giant flower
                the human poem

        walking through Dublin
            as Dublin
                walks through him.

## 30

When light sets eyes on rain one anxious evening
it loves and marries it against all the odds
as someone crippled in a bed of pain
is calmed-caressed by inescapable gods.

## 31

The man in the next bed
to Dermot Gillespie died
this wild flying October afternoon.
All of a slap, Gillespie was a different man
talking of his days in the army,
a gun in his hand,
knew how to use it.
'Know your enemies,' he hissed,
'Men are menaces if they're not disciplined.'

'What's not escape?' I asked.

'Nothing,' said the man of rain.

Nothing is the Four Courts, the Five Lamps,
the Nine Daughters' Hole, the spawning frog
in the bog, the gift of tulips,
the Ten Best Books of the Year.

What year, for God's sake? Why don't I
ask October? I do.

'I'm John the Baptist to the month of the dead,'
October says. 'This one is dying out.
So am I, ever since they named me.
October. I have my own colours.
I have a feeling for lovers, they come
and go through my cool rooms,
my testy fields, my melancholy words.
They stroll willingly into my nets,
some of them I capture forever
as if their presence in my colours
would soften the blow for the dying year,
one more dying year, like an old envelope
blown hither and thither through the streets
or along the edges of the canal.
No one will ever know what it contained.
All the dying years love
to have their hearts caressed by rain.
It feels like praise or cool forgiveness.
What do the dying years remember?
What do I, October, remember?
I like to think my colours touched November.'

I kissed October.

I reached out my left hand to the man of rain.
Some of my fingers were frozen.
Were they dry or bleeding?
Stones or feathers? Alive or dead?

'You'll never escape October,' he said.

## 32

I looked into his crying eyes, how can
the rain be crying?
It is. Rain sheds itself, sheds tears as well,
the tears are running down his face
yet do not fall to earth.

This helps me to talk, he said.

Me too, I said.

Talk to me, he said.

I'm crying because I'm not afraid,
I said, and I thought I would be.
Fear came to me last night
and slept beside me.
Please let me stay, it said,
please let me lie with you
and live in you,

I want to thrive in you,
to make my own of you,
don't throw me out,
I'll have to spend tonight in some stranger's heart,
I like your heart, bad an' all as it is,
let me take up residence there,
I'll be a decent tenant, I'll earn my keep,
pay my way, what does your old heart say?

I'm a callous bastard at times.

Get out of here, I said, out of my bed,
out of my heart, g'wan, take to the roads,
hit the streets, find another heart to live in,
you're not welcome here.

You should have seen the face of fear,
all black passionate disappointment,
black as oily scrags of sand
on Sandymount Strand.

Fear doesn't like me anymore,
since I sent it slinking out the door.
It's left a deep space in my heart.
I'll put music there instead,
I'm crying, I can't stop crying,
you're crying too, man of rain. Why?

There are only so many ways to die, he said.
The way without fear is good.
I dislike evictions but I evicted fear
from my rain, what you call blood.
This eviction tells me who I am.
I'm a man made of rain, simply that,
only that. My rain is music, can you hear it?
I'll put music in my heart, you said.
It's already there.
Listen. Open your deep space.
Let your music out, let my music in.
The world is a closed shell.
Prise it open with your tears.
Fear is hell, get out of hell.

His eyes were pouring now, no longer crying,
he was rain that doesn't cry but pours
understanding on the frozen
witness of our fear.

Let my music in, he said again, let
my music fill the empty space,
will you let it in?

I'll try, I said, and couldn't explain
the sudden shiver in my stomach, the quick
nail in my forehead. Had I told
the truth? Had I lied?

The wall of my chest opened, bloody unholy door.

I went inside.

I want to tell him I've been robbed of words
but none exist for me to say.
Waking this morning
I could name nothing.
Name. Nothing.

What's the meaning of dulcet, Scruffy?
Scruffy Grace never heard of dulcet.
He'll pay for it.
Four on either hand.

Scruffy. Dulcet. Scruffy Grace.
Words so strange they paralyse your tongue.

Four slaps on either hand.
Slaps.
Shlaps.
Four shlaps on either hand
burning the line of joy, the line of sorrow.

Frig him, and his dulcet,
Scruffy spits after school, cooling
his hands at the fountain, what do I
know about dulcet, a lot o' bloody good
dulcet'll do me on a London buildin' site,
I never heard anyone around here
sayin' dulcet this or dulcet that,
dulcet father or mother
or bread or butter
or creamery-milk,
to hell with friggin dulcet,
let me outa here.

Scruffy got outa there
and hit the London building-site,
pick and shovel in the outcast light
and thirty quid a week, a fortune.

Fifty years on, it's all I have :
Scruffy Grace. Dulcet. A fortune.

I can't even say them.
They say me, over and over
and over.
The flesh becomes a word.

What's an eyelid? What's a fingernail?
A human face?

What's a pick? What's a shovel?
A cement factory in Houghton Regis?

There, at the foot of the bed, the face of rain
          looking.

Somewhere in my brain, I say words:

              face

                    of

                          rain.

    I recognise

              the face

                    of rain.

# 34

My mind ran away from me
                    down the hill of blood
and I ran after it
                    calling 'Come back! Come back!'

but my mind turned and laughed in my face
as it joined a fox in a merry dash
on a sudden green run of the hill.
Then it turned and ran towards me,
laughing all the while because that
is my mind's style if it can be said
to have a style.
'You silly old lump of cotton wool,' it said,
'Why should I bother to live in you,
you damp old house full of stuffy furniture,
you've no idea what fun it is
to escape from you
and run in the living air.
So many sprightly minds are trapped in the heads
of tedious old things like you.'

            I couldn't answer that, I was
mindless at the time, still am
            but I have something else –

a driven thing, a force, a rip, a kick,
a lick, a bite, a wandering, a honing-in,
a taste for things hurtfully sudden and quick
and the heaven-hellish out-of-it
                    view of things

you get when you're bloody sick.

# 35

There's an irony at work I cannot fathom
shining in the sunlit pigeon shit
dripping from the battlements of the castle
where all is useless that is not a plot

or part of a plot. This clean winter day
can't stop the stink of treachery
filling the city: treachery of the dead
against the living, then turn it round,

history is now. Right. Wrong. Sing dumb.
There's an irony at work I cannot fathom.

You never had a penny so let your kingdom come.


# 36

Amor stares at the long black rib of
        hair on the floor,
at the big black suicide slab near
        the Gallery door,
at students passing. Which of them
        will come home
from a birthday party and hang herself
        in her own bedroom?

'Gather yourself, we'll go to the cold,' he invited.

'It must be blue,' I said.

'Why do you put a colour on everything?' he asked.

'There's nothing without a colour,' I replied.

'The cold I'm going to show you has no colour,' he said.

We sat in Saint Stephen's Green, calm as you like,
but the Green and everyone in it
lifted into the sky
and there was Dublin below, far below.
I saw me getting off the train at Kingsbridge,
it was nineteen fifty-four, Manning murdered
the nurse in a field near Limerick
but John the beggar told me fifty years later
Manning didn't mean it, he got carried away
by heaven between her legs and strangled her
and was hanged, the last man to be hanged
by the law in Ireland, hanged in the Joy, John the beggar
played handball with Manning the day before
he got strung up, and all Manning wanted
was a prayer over his limestone grave
which John gave to God before he was released
to stand on the Halfpenny Bridge with his cap
in his hand, the cap stretched out, his head down,
the most humble bleedin' man in Dublin, he said,
that's what they love, the bit o' humility,
that's the boy to stir their charity,
well by Jaysus they have their man, if it's
humility they want I'll give 'em capfuls of it
and I made thirteen pounds and four pence
the first day I stood on the Halfpenny Bridge,
more than many's the Civil Servant made in his office,
beggin' the eyes o' the passers-by, my head down,
my hands cold, my heart warm at the thought
of what turned out to be thirteen pounds and four pence.
For some men, prison is the start o' common sense.

Never commit a crime again, Manning said,
never rob a tourist or steal timber from buildin'-sites,
beg your way to a sound sleep every night
and when you lie between a woman's legs
try not to strangle her or you'll finish up
in a limestone grave and who
will throw an ould prayer to God for you?
From the edge of my grave I beg you be wise
and you'll never feel the cold of an ould judge's eyes.
I looked down into Dublin, I thought I saw
pain and laughter in the eyes
of the man made of rain
but I wouldn't swear to it.
Down there, Dublin was a star in the womb of time,
it was having a hard time being born, remember
the man who said Dublin
is an Empire's abortion, but to me 'twas a star, just then,
shining below, so far below,
the only star whose light
shone upwards
on men, women, children,
shone upwards
like a stray, impossible prayer from hell.

One day you see a woman, one day you don't,
she vanishes, you never even knew her name,
I saw the girl from the Isle of Wight
on a bicycle in Ship Street,
then she was gone into a bath
shoving a clothes hanger up herself,
I'd cherish her name if I knew it, I think the greyfaced man
on the cobbles was the father of what
the clothes hanger tried to polish off,
but the girl died instead, her blue eyes
laughing still
in the guinnessy smoke of O'Neills.
Suppose she can feel, what is it she feels?
How cold is she now, after thirty years?

When I asked these questions I saw them sinking
into the eyes of the man made of rain,
ice now, but kind for all that, kind ice
if that's not too much to swallow,

the kindest ice you'd ever dare to touch,
it was entering me, this cold
was taking me over, so cold, pure possession,
so cold I didn't feel cold any more
and never would again, it seemed,
I didn't even think of it, you think of it only
when you're humancold, or halfcold,
or cold enough to shiver or weep,
that's when you feel it, that's when you say
'I'm cold'.

But I was not.

Gone beyond it, gone
into
blue, I would say.

A bit like the kind of goodbye
you will never describe to anyone,
but let me say there was a white door
and herself
and goodbye
and splitting forever and maybe for good
and that walk by the poisoned Irish Sea
gifting cancer to children
like an evil Santa who'll never rest
till the cries fill his blood
and he sinks to rest
like a malignant sun drowned in the West.

How cold is a drowning sun?

Pluck it out of the heavens
drown it in the poisoned seas
of the world of men who never have time
to sit in Stephen's Green
and gaze at Dublin
from an altitude hard to believe
but easy so easy to love.

It was the first time I looked down
at the sun.

It was floundering, gasping,
struggling to light, dying to shine,
drowning.

It was the first time I saw the sun drowning.

'Save it,' I cried to the man made of rain.

He did.

I looked. The sun was over my head.

Thanks be to God, I said, that's the right place for it.

How long will it be
till all the seas
are one poisoned sea

and what'll we call it then?

She's gone forever
behind the white door.

It's cold, this side of the white door,
so cold it's four o'clock in the morning,
five ducks squatting on the dark waters of the canal,
light in the darkness of water a privilege, a woman
talking to herself on Baggot Street Bridge,
a man cycling so slowly it might be
a summer's day with men gathering hay
in a sweating meadow, houses asleep now
in the freezing nightlight, Joe Tandy bundled up
in *Heralds* and *Independents* in the doorway
of Superquinn, the streets unmolested by people
except myself and other sleepless things, the statue
of Oscar Wilde nice an' lazy in Merrion Square,
cold enough for every window of Holles Street
Hospital to be shut tight as tomorrow or
the old judge's mind to Manning all swaddled in limestone,
streets beckoning, opening up like veins
I must go through again and again, cold
as they were in the eighteenth century
of classic beauty, heroic couplets, Penal Laws,

handsome houses becoming perfect slums,
cold of history, cold facts, can't dispute them,
the statues are there to prove whatever
statues prove, how cold is Oliver Goldsmith
this morning, how cold is Edmund Burke,
how cold is the man made of rain?

The edge of the scythe is cold
the lips of my father's corpse are cold
winter mud is cold
the silence of splitting is cold
the white door is cold.

He flowed beside me.

'You can't even shiver,' he said.
'Ill teach you to shiver again.
I'll teach you to weep.
Shiver and weep.
Are you ready to learn?'

'I'm not cold,' I said.

'You don't feel cold?' he queried.

'No.'
'That's the cold I want you to know,' he said.
'The cold you cannot feel
or will not feel
or do not dare to feel.'

'If I can't feel it
how can I know it?' I asked.

'Trust me,' he said. 'Will you trust me?'

'Into the belly of eternity,' I replied.
'But how can I know?'

He smiled. 'When you are me.'

'When's that?'

'How shall we clean the sea?'

'Don't ask me. The thought of it is enough…
to make me… make me…'

'To make you shiver?'

'Yes.'

'You must be cold.'

'Yes. With anger, bafflement, a block
of icy rage'.

'Good. It's time to go back down
to Dublin town, there's no cold like the cold
of not knowing how cold the heart has grown'.

'What are we doing up here?' I asked.

'Strolling through Stephen's Green,' he replied.

'I'd almost forgotten,' I said.
'Where have we been?'

'Looking down at the drowning sun
Listening to the sun's death-rattle.
That's all.'

The man made of rain looked at the sky.
Darkwhite. Coldwet. Sharp blue light,
the kind that makes me feel I'm free,
the sun in its proper place, as far as I could see,
not far, but far enough for me.

He began to walk away.
'Goodbye for now,' he said. 'You'll sleep tonight.'

He swallowed, or was swallowed by
the trueblue light.

## 38

Many a man carries a lunatic asylum
on his neck and shoulders
and has the gumption to call it his head.
'You could be returning into what they call
the real world,' he said.
'The real people are waiting for you
to judge, advise, prophesy, explain.
That's the goodness of the heart.
The real people know the truest language
and the most effective way to think.
Depart from that, you're in
the provinces of lost,
the diaspora of the bucking moon.
But don't worry, you'll be with
the real people soon.'

There's an irony at work I cannot fathom.
You never had a penny so let your kingdom come.

'I know I'm going back,' I said
'along the Via Blackrockia
via Sandycove and Dalkey
and the waves of Bullock Harbour
to the real world
where the devil has a mobile phone
and God a walkie-talkie.'

'Don't forget to change your trousers,' he said,
'Your arse is peeking out
like an astounded face
witnessing the first copulation
of Adam and Eve
in the shade of the old appletree
in that blameless tempting paradisal place
where they paid no rent
until they stalked each other with foul intent.'

'How do I know the time to leave,
to reach the real world,' I asked.

'Your father'll tell you.'

'He's dead.'

'Your father'll tell you.'

'Will I ever see you again?'
'You will.'

'Where?'

'I'll be pouring down and around
in your bucking head.'

'And how long will you stay
pouring
down and around
in my bucking head?'

'How long would you like?'

'Until the end.'

'The end happened before you were born
but if you believe there's an end to come,
I'll stay.'

'You'll stay? In the real world? Why?'

'Say I could be your friend.'

# 39

Pain has a weather of its own
Pain knocks at the skull and slips in
Pain smiles at the child and hovers
Pain can be shy and then turn Hitler
Pain aches for a place in my heart
and who am I to deny it?

## 40

There's a small room between remembering and forgetting
where tulips live longer
than in most other rooms.
I don't own it, it doesn't own me,
it allows me to remember and forget
as I will, as they will.
It is bare and welcoming, in its way,
nobody is ever there to stay, including me.
This is what it means to be free.
Remember that. Forget it.
Free is a million ways, a wild style,
one way is enough for the moment
and would I know freedom if I
met it in the street?

Pain turns memory into a flood
of knowledge and ignorance.
This flood is the reason for the dance.
If I can't answer the question, Who is God?
I'm for the stick.
Children need the stick, Mulcahy said.
It's the stick that makes 'em dance.
It's the dance that makes 'em happy.

Rosie Keogh throws her bicycle
on the side of the road, September blackberries,
points towards the graveyard and says
'That fella Yeats is buried in there.
They all laughed at him around here.
He believed in the fairies.'

Two miles outside Banagher, Corrigan turns his car
and drives back.
The road is wet, he steps on the gas.
''Tis twenty to eight,' he mutters,
'and I didn't get
my Lotto ticket yet.
This could be my night.'

Galvin's wife is half-woman, half-man.
He found out on his wedding night.
He was a sad eejit after that.
Never allowed to forget.
They sniggered at him in the street.

So what if I remember
what never happened
but is more vicious or foolish in memory
than if it had?
Deceives, animates, wearies me as well.
Memory laughs all the way to hell.

I look into the eyes of the man of rain.
I will not say I know what I see.
I will not remember, I will not forget,
I will let
whatever happens
happen to me,
I will let
what I know of the happy dance
lie down with my agony.

After that, I'll see.

# 41

'Come back! Please come back!' I begged my mind
'And I promise I'll behave.'
'Behave!' my mind spat, 'Didn't I just see you
rambling up and down your father's grave!'

'Is that all you saw?' I asked. 'Yes,' darted my mind,
'I saw what could be seen, it was perfectly clear.'
'There was more to it than that,' I said. 'You sick nut,'
rapped my mind, 'Shut up! I'm getting out of here!'

My mind took off down the hill of blood
running full pelt through the morning.
It looked back once, saw a real sick nut
seeing a bright, informed, frightened thing.

# 42

I see the wounded sky
    this bluebright morning
        (such cold, such network cold)

and though the sky is bleeding
    the wound, slowly and shyly,
        begins to sing

filling the silent trenches
    above the witnessing counties,
        above my right and wrong,

above money and killing
    and sacredly useless poetry
        faltering into song.

The wound reaches the sun,
    reassures it as it
        hangs trembling

over Dublin and graffiti
    proclaiming
        fiercely secret loving

and gas couplings in Killarney Street.
    The grateful sun accepts
        the wound's comforting

touch, shining, exploring
    corners it has ignored    forgotten
        since Eden morning.

The wound of love's the most living thing
    in mugging streets of greed.
        I watch it bleeding

there where wings come clattering
    to my window,
        raindrops glittering

like jewels flung to celebrate
    the wound's bloodwonder,
        mild thunder in my heart and head

as I move all of me
    to drop on the waiting windowsill
        small bits of bread.

# 43

'Say I could be your friend.'

I brought that back from the jungle.

'What do you mean?' I asked.

'If your scars are made of fear, tell me,' he said.
'If there's anything you fear to say, tell me.
Pour all you are and think and feel and dream
into my rain. Telling is learning to drown
in my rain. Say I could be your friend.
Mankind. Do you like that word? These words?
Man. Kind. I like to go raining in the jungle.'

'I like to walk the streets,' I said.

'Could be you will again,' he said.
'Why do you like walking the streets?'

'Variety,' I replied. 'Faces. Eyes. Smiles. Half-smiles.
Averted eyes. Thin, wispy perfumes of fear.
Whatever points to something I've met somewhere
in the jungle under the skin.'

I looked at him. For the first time, I looked closely
at his heart of rain.
My heart was beating again
like the hearts of those in the real world.
His heart of rain beat too, a rhythm
planets imitate and stars will dance to,
neglected, far stars dancing
in the high wide stage of the sky.
Anne-Marie loves Buffo. I read that
scrawled on a wall. Ann-Marie is shy.
Buffo doesn't know. Dance with me, Buffo.
Dance with Ann-Marie.

The rain in his heart is not straight down
but slanting, firm, clear and clean.
The rain on Dublin
has a special poison
but the rain in his heart
is the heavens' own rain.

I want to walk in it, I want to walk
through the rain
in the heart of the man of rain.
He looks at me, reads my obvious brain.

'Come on,' he said 'Walk through my heart.'

Ann-Marie is shy. Dance with me, Buffo.

I'm walking through his heart,
a heart my heart says will not harbour lies,
unlike mine.

Such light, such dancing light, such clear skies.
His rain is pouring through my eyes,
tired years are falling out of my eyes,
falling at my feet, the rain falls on them,
God in heaven, swans in the canal,
these years are turning fresh again,
I hope someone comes along and finds them,
in the heart of rain I know I can share
anything with anyone, in the heart of rain
love is particular and fluent, why am I
talking about love, I never knew much
about it for Christ's sake, it's falling
all around, through me, it wants to live,
what's killing it, don't ask, I never knew
much about it, glimpses of love when love
didn't know I was looking, or did it, does love know
all about lookers-on, does it take pity
on eyes that speak impoverished hearts,
on hearts afraid to love, on hearts
that die for want of telling in the heart of rain,
I'm walking now, this heart is endless,
it stretches away as far as I believe

I see, and farther, farther than the suckling
whale making it from warm Mexico
to freezing waters eleven thousand miles away,
farther than that, walking through rain,
cool joy, happy dance, Ann-Marie loves Buffo,
walking through this heart that's beating
for the stars' pleasure and my soul's poverty,
this heart is fun, is lightning, is what makes the Atlantic
wild and mighty for a worker in September
when it's time to say thank you to the sun
for work well done, the harvest won,
I'm walking still, something is having mercy
on me, walking where a dream might flag,
some things are wilder than the wildest dream,

I'm walking in the hills that tap their feet
for dancing streets that I will walk again,
I hope, I hope, this moment living in the heart of rain,
heart of the man of rain, no lies, no lies tonight,
such light, such dancing light, clear skies.

Where is he?

Foot of the bed.

Where am I?

Here. Lying here.

Why am I dreaming of streets?

He's silent now, I walked through his heart,
will he ever speak to me again,
how must he feel, now that I've trampled his heart?

I make to close my eyes, they're already closed.

The tide is in.

Talk to me, man of rain.

I love you.

Anne-Marie loves Buffo. That love
is writ on heaven's floor
on a wall in Protestant Row
off Wexford Street
in Dublin.

Hard to imagine myself walking again
but if I do
I'll study the signs, consider the evidence,
wondering

what did they do with all that blood,
wondering

which way will I go, which street, which road?
Will he be there?
Will he come again?

Will he lead me where
my dreams won't venture?
What is the cost
of being privileged and lost?

                  I thank
                     the heart of sickness

                  for the man of rain

laughing away from me
   returning
      slipping through me
         like a needle
            a word
               morning ice
                  memory blitz
                     a knife
               with a mind of its own
                     to stab
                        cut
                     and save
                        my life

                  that, after sixty years,
                     I wonder at
                     know little about
                        sitting here
watching pigeons invigorate themselves
   beaks working breast and back and wing
      before they test the hardy air
         of this March morning.

**Brendan Kennelly** was born in 1936 in Ballylongford, Co. Kerry; and was educated at St Ita's College, Tarbert, Co. Kerry, and at Trinity College, Dublin, where he has been Professor of Modern Literature since 1973. He has published more than twenty books of poems, including *My Dark Fathers* (1964), *Collection One: Getting Up Early* (1966), *Good Souls to Survive* (1967), *Dream of a Black Fox* (1968), *Love Cry* (1972), *The Voices* (1973), *Shelley in Dublin* (1974), *A Kind of Trust* (1975), *Islandman* (1977), *A Small Light* (1979) and *The House That Jack Didn't Build* (1982). *The Boats Are Home* (1980) is still available from Gallery Press and *Moloney Up and At It* from the Mercier Press. His latest book is *The Man Made of Rain* (Bloodaxe Books, 1998).

He is best-known for two controversial poetry books, *Cromwell*, published in Ireland in 1983 and in Britain by Bloodaxe in 1987, and his epic poem *The Book of Judas*, which topped the Irish bestsellers list when it was published by Bloodaxe in 1991. His third epic, *Poetry My Arse* (Bloodaxe, 1995), may outdo these in notoriety.

His books of poems translated from the Irish include *A Drinking Cup* (Allen Figgis, 1970) and *Mary* (Aisling Press, Dublin 1987), and his translations are now collected in *Love of Ireland: Poems from the Irish* (Mercier Press, 1989). He has edited several anthologies, including *The Penguin Book of Irish Verse* (1970; 2nd edition 1981), *Between Innocence and Peace: Favourite Poems of Ireland* (Mercier Press, 1993), *Ireland's Women: Writings Past and Present*, with Katie Donovan and A. Norman Jeffares (Gill & Macmillan, 1994), and *Dublines*, with Katie Donovan (Bloodaxe Books, 1995). He has published two novels, *The Crooked Cross* (1963) and *The Florentines* (1967).

He is also a celebrated dramatist whose plays include versions of *Antigone* (Peacock Theatre, Dublin, 1986; Bloodaxe, 1996); *Medea*, premièred in the Dublin Theatre Festival in 1988, toured in England in 1989 by the Medea Theatre Company, and broadcast by BBC Radio 3 and published by Bloodaxe in 1991; *The Trojan Women* (Peacock Theatre & Bloodaxe, 1993); and Lorca's *Blood Wedding* (Northern Stage, Newcastle & Bloodaxe, 1996).

His *Journey into Joy: Selected Prose*, edited by Åke Persson, was published by Bloodaxe in 1994, along with *Dark Fathers into Light*, a critical anthology on his work edited by Richard Pine. Åke Persson has also published *That Fellow with the Fabulous Smile: A Tribute to Brendan Kennelly* (Bloodaxe, 1996).

Brendan Kennelly has published six volumes of selected poems, most recently *A Time for Voices: Selected Poems 1960-1990* (Bloodaxe, 1990) and *Breathing Spaces: Early Poems* (Bloodaxe, 1992).